T0046521

"CM Burroughs's *Master Suffering* is transce
vulnerability, and a guttural beauty. The nu
treatise on bereavement and belief, is a younger sister's death.
Often employing the epistolary as a form of elegy, *Master Suffering*
investigates the labyrinthine dimensions of desire, mourning,
faith, and misogyny. The keening power of Burroughs' poems is
felt repeatedly, especially in the stripped down interrogative, 'Why
would you put / so much sadness in one person?' Ultimately,
Master Suffering serves as a concentrated 'balancing song'—a book-
length conjuring to counter grief's entropy. It is a pulsing utterance
providing solace in the dark."

SIMONE MUENCH

"Dear reader, I would stop us at the title of this harrowing and
beautifully ranging book, and have us note how that title—*Master
Suffering*—sits, on one hand, as imperative and, on another, as a nod
to old suffering's power over all of us. The book goes deeply into the
territories—death and family and the various ways bodies fail us and
also 'radiant pain opening/ as pure sound.' And note, dear reader,
the gestures toward order, these in the epistolary riffs (complete with
trigger warnings) and in the repeated insistence on cleaning house.
And note that liver, site of the organ failure addressed here, is also
the word for one who lives. Halfway in, CM Burroughs writes, 'I have
seen myself through.' There's so much here."

C. S. GISCOMBE

"*Master Suffering*: a directive? Or a direct address? CM Burroughs
throws us off-balance before we've opened the cover of her dynamic
new collection, and continues to blow us away, moving us further and
more deeply with each turn of the page. The voice in these poems
echoes with wrenching questions ('Ready to suffer?' 'Do you want to
look inside?'), although its assertions speak just as resonantly: 'I will
suffer desire,' she writes in one poem. 'I have seen myself through,'
in another. Burroughs opens a door for her reader onto a world of

emotion contained by hospital corners and taut lines; we are invited in, though not as passive onlookers, but 'active participant[s]': 'Fit your body into the [].' What do grief, sex, and poetry have in common? The 'arc through pain to (is it?) pleasure.' Travel this terrain of blurred boundaries with Burroughs until all lines—except the lines of these amazing poems—dissolve."

EVIE SHOCKLEY

"CM Burroughs's *Master Suffering* is a striking, brave, and stunning book. Her poems consider the problem of the body, the woman's body in particular, and the speaker's bravery with sex, with being in a body, and lusting after life. This desire or impulse is contraposed with the story of her sister, who died following a rejected liver transplant. There is a physicality or muscularity of these body poems that is heightened by a third thread, a questioning, of the Creator, of authority figures, ghosts, voices in one's own head, etc. These don't necessarily have answers, but they try to tie together the other two: the vibrant, sexual-feeling, free person and the memory, of the gone person whose body couldn't have that. Her forms are so beautiful and they really reinforce the content and ideas in the poems. There are fragments, tremendous leaps, epistles, some like cries in the dark, and others are more like exclamations. I love Burroughs's poems and I love *Master Suffering*. It's not easy to make poems like these, and they are important."

SEAN SINGER

MASTER SUFFERING

MASTER SUFFERING
Poems

CM Burroughs

TUPELO PRESS

2021

Master Suffering
Copyright © 2021 CM Burroughs. All rights reserved.

Library of Congress LCCN: 2020943368
ISBN-13: 978-1-946482-38-9

Cover image: Anonymous, American, 20th century.
Cover and text design by adam b. bohannon.

First paperback edition January 2021

All rights reserved. Other than brief excerpts for reviews and commentaries, no part of this book may be reproduced by any means without permission of the publisher. Please address requests for reprint permission or for course-adoption discounts to:

Tupelo Press
P.O. Box 1767
North Adams, Massachusetts 01247
(413) 664-9611 / Fax: (413) 664-9711
editor@tupelopress.org / www.tupelopress.org

Tupelo Press is an award-winning independent literary press that publishes fine fiction, non-fiction, and poetry in books that are a joy to hold as well as read. Tupelo Press is a registered 501(c)(3) non-profit organization, and we rely on public support to carry out our mission of publishing extraordinary work that may be outside the realm of the large commercial publishers. Financial donations are welcome and are tax deductible.

This project is supported in part by an award from the National Endowment for the Arts.

for my mother, father, and brother—who keep me aloft.

CONTENTS

Are you a woman or a mouse?
Annie Dillard

And what shall we do, those of us who did not die?
June Jordan

The Lovers

This time they form a cross on
the kitchen table as he stands
before her skyward navel savors
her wilding curls and restrains
his end for what bird breathes
between them.

She marries her hands
to the bends of his stomach,
sucks air and suspends it
for the eclipse that stuns.

He looks down on her body
effacing the simple table, says
Yes Yes and they've left

the curtains chasmal
liking the parabolic backlight,
liking being seen.

He is gifting her
his patience and tills her
nerves soundless. No one said
it could be like this:

returning your partner's gaze,
learning his whole language,
realizing you, too, can be read.

To Be in Love

Call it bondage   blue lake girding my

       wrists and viscera

swell under plum   hood of skin

Call it vernissage   harness

       spotlight

I feel what you make   in your imagination

bleakness blackness   any animal nosing air

       What do you desire?

My hanging here   My serum's burgeoning

gape Beautiful   half-golden hurt

       salted in sweat

My love I want   to be rigged

Body as a Juncture of Almost

It is female. It is girl parts.
       Ready to suffer? Predilection for.
Ready to try to live? I tell it— how
       I became what I am. Not forgiving
of myself, but forgetting
       the irrational start. Why
should I have wanted so much
       as to threaten my being?
Refusal to recall what I was (the
       impossibility of this) for three months
captured in a clear box

       (look: [the clear box])

my trying to be. Self that I own.
I own her. At least.

II.

Joy is/is a syllable down the causeway yet unlit.
The speakers keep saying it is so. Argue. Say:
capture her and her in the midst of gesture,
between desire and satisfaction—. See: stutter of
woman; breasts and bone between wanting to
have and having, the irrevocably rote discomfort
between.

III.

I want you to understand what this bracket feels like: [ ]

Be an active participant in the difficult narrative

of body. Fit your body into the [ ]

IV.

Are you reading what I am handing you? My
body   hinged to the Other.   Hyphen.

Do you think about her kneecaps and arched spine, her
navel and clavicle, her whole?

Do you want
to look inside?

V.

I don't want you to hurt, but

watch her understand what it is; watch her arc through pain to (is it?)
pleasure. Something from which she doesn't want to run   (stay put in)

                                   meter of organ and sense. What now it
                                   feels like to be touched. Like *this*. Again
                                   like *this*.

VI.

Watch her (look at me) so much

       a woman now, parabola
       and experience, muscles at ease

with want and its yield.

       You will need so much empathy to
       feel her feeling.

Questions During Protest

are rhetorical and involve ownership: he possesses every thing: his body and mine; gives fill-ins for me to say "yes, yours, yes." Exactly.

"I am an offering" is my unwinding, where—plat after dampened plat —I disband. Ordinary questions carousel my wrists and ankles. I name often my parts to clarify the   object my body.

I undress my courteous bones, helix patiently. See each balking scar's variant pattern. What you're hurting for puts a hurt on you, my hips' serum quelling your hum.

I've not said *syncretic form*, my idea for staving touch; syllables biding in my pink throat. I spread each expandable part, wanting you to see how cleanly I am. What muscle over what hinging gestural box. All of what I am—holding.

Before Autopsy

To put my hands into her body will mean to be overcome, so that I am black or all that I will say is "black," because it hasn't a name.

I am overcome because it is unnamed and I want to call it. I call it and want for it, hymn and rivet, to come. I will suffer desire; suffer it.

The Wait

Love's the rosarian lengthwise on the pallet, welt in remnants of
damask rose, hive, and vellum wings. Love's the duvet built in
honey and—blessing by cardinals' breasts—
     the woman intent on tending her good man.

Her goldenrod navel, draught for feeding, draws in under
touch then opens as eye. Irises are shadows of
musculature: the bent of abdominals, obliques, and
pelvic slope. Arbor of asters, her center, a
     conservatory of light, undress to lathe.

Incidents for the Forgettery

After I scour the kitchen to the alleys
of the stove, ring and hang the wash,
disappear the garbage, bleach the bath,
perfect the bed, its strict corners,
he says, "it's nice to have another
adult around," which resonates
to the effect of: you are particular skin
I want to assuage, as in: won't you
stay with me forever?
What I mishear is the objective
hue of his voice, its inflection
signifying the wonder he holds for a
woman's functional use. I am welcome
for my utility, how I might serve, my
southern grace having grown me
toward the necessity of a tool.

Incidents for the Forgettery

My sister's body would be felled
by a ruinous liver the size of my
palm and positively
killing a whole person whom I'd spent
my life loving and protecting all the ways
one young body can protect another. I
wasn't always good, but I tried
my best to barter after missteps, after
hurting her good humor, and held
her hand until she was old enough not
to want me. If I could change anything,
I would have taken her place, ushered *her*
into syllable and verse. No liver
would have laid her low. Or I would have
plainly had her live, healthy from start to
finish, free of any organ's gross intents.

Incidents for the Forgettery

There were things I could not alter: the functional disorder
of my sister's body riddled by anonymous disease.
My faith dwelled in doctors' muster and machinery. I
shuddered what I did not know.

I cleaned for her returns from Emory, Chicago Children's, and
Johns Hopkins hospitals; I meditated on the dusting of wicker,
its intentional racks, and arranged artful dolls just so, just
so that she might cross comfort, models of ease in her home.

Is it any wonder I sank myself into duty? What else could be set right
at the insistence of my hand? When bearing into my training, I could
touch and turn matter into its most masterful self. My sister wasn't
made of such seams.

II

Most Beautiful Thing
for Doug

When I say I am patient, I mean that for some length of time, I did
not know myself, nor was I confident that I would be known.

(This was constantly my preoccupation.

Likely the preoccupation of any body
in a natural state of peril.)

My reasons being

I came early to the world and might have died.
I came early to the world and might have killed myself.
I came early to the world but missed my own passing.

It took years to find

I am blessed or impossibly fortunate.

I feel the life of my dead sister filling me.

I have seen myself through.

Supposition

for my mother

Let us admit there has been division enough; our teeth, its simplest
actors.

Let us admit
the *past*—our translucent bodies' betrayal: good natures' good
windows.

We were, weren't we, moveable?
Series of solid matters sected.

Mid-life and mothered, historical warnings hum, "Don't split the
pole—"

so as not to forget oneself   so as not to be beguiled by the
menagerie present.

For any seer, bisection percusses elemental:

tension then yoke attention
to see oneself   and one's companion starkly on *this* side of the
divining pine.

If you split the pole,

better to graft your error, better
to right your route than to risk

misfortune's unrelenting map. For your mother and her mother...

and hers. For the lot of us, the clot of us regarding
the unsteady water, unsteady water in

familial gourds at our feet.

Basic Training

for my father

I learned to clean house at age 10 under the
instruction of a U.S. Marine, my father,
teaching me that a job worth doing was a
job worth doing well. Task turned
meditation, my introversion
summoned space in redundant duties of house: ritual
rescuing of counters under day's crumb, esophageal kicks
of the hoover in hand,
hypnotic polishing of torchieres, side tables, and
talons from the hands and feet of mahogany chairs.
Lastly, I could sit and survey
my balancing song. It was gratifying: I could
set my mind to changing a thing, and it would
change.

Wean and Stop

I weaned from the antidepressant and my
system rebelled—I couldn't
keep anything down, not water,
no
solid thing, I lost
11 pounds in 8 weeks, and my body wasn't adjusting, which

frightened me because

       I had not known I was so dependent.

       I was afraid of what my body would do if I tried again.

       I was in hospital 6 times during the 2 months for
       dehydration, trying to sleep in the beds of ERs
       with an IV in my arm.

Once I guessed weaning had made me sick, I
took the pill and felt
fine, as in
"normal," within hours.

If nothing else, *that* was crazy.

Dear Liver,

Grant that you are part of the capsule of her. You are integral to the
system of her and have one function—to clean.

> Which you were made for, which was assigned you
> at the beginning of time.

What can be said that will help you to understand
the values of your labor? So much depends upon the figure you cut

> in the bantam cage of her body,
> yourself dwarfing every other meat.

You are the namer of things, fitful when not fair, and decide what to
refine, deterge, and tender back to blood.

> I look to you without looking.
> I apologize, my poor inner eye.

Dear Liver,

Most times she had to be held down, moored

to the bed so medicine could
bend in her blood. Her body, raw with heat,
resolved against your resonant wings.

How did you see yourself then? How
urgently did you come to your calling
or hers?

Incidents for The Forgettery

She understood gravity as offertory and sometimes slept that way.
Preferable to pain was the numbing of her calves, ankles, and feet.
Right angled to the wall, the migration of blood yielded relief.

Dear Liver,

      How many times, once we knew the culprit,
did we curse the bad liver of her birth, or the second—a
gift, eager to escape the capsule of her—double-lobed
brute disrupting in plumes.

      Given all the prayers against the organs' recurrent
failure, God became further debatable.

God Letter

If I could think of Him as formless, all energy and myth,

                I could believe better. Dear Van

thank you for saying that spirituality explains

                what science can't. This makes

sense to me, mostly because I needed language

                that worked outside

figures mimicking the human form, i.e. God and

                Jesus. Does spirituality exist

at the end of knowledge? It was you who told me

                Einstein didn't believe

in a personal God, but in "Spinoza's God who reveals

                himself in the orderly harmony

of what exists," which makes me think of nature

                poetry, how harmony, to borrow

the word, can occur. And I-know-I-know-the-writer

                -as-God, but skipping that

I am impressed by Einstein permitting himself

                multitudes, space to critique

one belief and occupy another. I have never

                understood religion as liberated

but as rigid order of ritual, and the force of Him

                is powerful in the Baptist church

where I grew up—Van, what I find important is

                your desire to learn and your openness

to spirituality; it is lush and teaches me, too,

                to be a scholar of belief, an informed

believer—if I should come to that.

God Letter

A body creating bodies happens everyday; it *is* female. Dear Fred,
the story about your daughter still makes me smile. Getting Pearl

into the princess towel club at camp is meaningful, especially if
she hates it once she's in. It's a shame she has to have something

special to join—beyond herself, I mean.
The memory of you two drawing princesses on white towels in

bright markers will keep her longer than a swath of girls. Better
to have something her own that can't be ghosted away.

The colors bled, which is completely art; I'll bet Pearl was radiant and
understood her fine parentage then. Groups are an invention

of the womb—to whom do I belong? And there are always rules,
which is the tough swallow, hinging to one's monumental sleeve.

God Letter

Do I have to dress up or can I wear jeans? Dear Joaquin,
casual Sunday is a plus ~ can a woman be fully present in heels?
Remember the other day at the shops, we saw the t-shirt that read
"Blessed" across the front? I know

you picked it up for me as a joke, but it made me pause. I think I am
blessed in the way *I* understand people to mean it: having good
fortune. But this is where faith messes with my clean concept, because
practicing Christians don't believe blessings come

out the clear blue sky. So here's God again, all up in the Kool-aid.
I'm dating myself, but I mean that He gets in the way of spiritual
minimalism. He is at once contained and uncontainable, which,
intellectually, is hard to understand. So being blessed

must require that one acts in such a way that presses God to bestow
blessings, which isn't the same thing as good fortune, but I want
to believe that people are saying "you have such good fortune, I
hope for good fortune, too," because it means that no one is

preaching at me like, "You have good God-God," "Father God, I
hope you God for us, too," "Go with God," Etcetera.

God Letter

       Forgive me. I have been
so very small-minded.
              Dear Sascha, I see you
sketching Jehovah's unknowable hand, how He
extends His perhaps palm in probable gesture,
stitches figmented fingers from their natural sieve
and sweeps   sweeps until this world is again,
again elemental.

Such that the President doesn't matter, the assault
on abortion rights doesn't matter, the negative
impact of climate change/disparity of wealth and
economic opportunity/child abuse/red-lining and
systemic racism/gender bias/misogyny doesn't
matter—
          minerals for new soil. By your hand, He sows

the dead in amended Midwestern plains, seals tungsten
mines, disappears nuclear clinker, commits full erasure.
And you—what comes first? Food? Water? Shelter?
Start small, smaller; plot the most basic of needs.

            Witnesses must have thought
waiting for the beginning was the patient part, the
anxiety of time, time enough, to be chosen as good,
as godly, but here you are reborn to the naked world
under strain of knowing what had been, deciding
with throngs of worthy acolytes what's to come next.

God Letter

Everybody is doing trigger warnings now, so
To Whom It May Concern, I hated God when
my sister died. I didn't know it was
coming, but we were at the hospital in a private
room for family, and our pastor
was there, the one who baptized me, and
he said Let us pray, and I kept my eyes
open to watch everybody, but
listened, and when he said Sometimes
God has to take back his angels,
I was smart enough to know, I was 16, that he
was saying she was gone or going
and I loathed him so much, he didn't see
the look on my face, that blazing anger
blank heart f-you-forever look, but then my
parents told us we were going to
take her off life support, and I died then,
and after they took away the machines we had
solitude, family time the five of us, mom,
dad, me, my brother, and my sister. Holding her
body she was warm she wasn't conscious
but she could hear us I know it, then they
opened the door for other family to
say goodbye and I was hugging her back
in her bed, my face against her face, my tears
wetting her cheek it was flush and her waving
hair, I wanted to hold her forever I was hurting
but felt selfish like other people wanted to say
goodbye too so I let go,

and her head kind of tilted to the side and
I straightened it so was a mess then
goodbye goodbye we left there to clean
the house for mourners to come.

God Letter

I thought something was wrong with me. Dear God, I
hid my grief, usually closed behind the door of my
bedroom closet, but also under my covers at night
where I was sure to quiet my sobbing because
I really quit composure and said grief Go and
There it was pulling me to myself and I didn't
talk about it, so when 5 years then 8 passed and I was still
grieving sometimes in the middle of the day
or walking to work, I finally went to see someone
and though she wouldn't tell me for months, she would
diagnose me with Major Depressive Disorder, and I
wouldn't believe it until I realized no one else in my family
was still in so much pain and I had thought about killing
myself because I was so much inconsolable
like the time I saw nothing in the road then ran broadside
into a bright red truck totaling my car but walking away, or
one evening in the library parking lot where I escaped after
dinner to weep, or the time when I considered
veering into the opposite lane but thinking about those other
people stopped me and there I was sobbing again for having
considered it and I went to my parents and said I think
something is wrong with me I can't stop crying and think about
killing myself and they said You have to get outside of yourself,
which wasn't wrong, I had always been an introvert,
but I would keep on the same way for years, through a therapist
or two, one who was a family friend and had known
my sister, who had me pay for my sessions myself I was 19,
it was $1 per session for me to feel empowered in my
healing, and he told me to hug my mother and
tell her I love her and I did. Why would you put
so much sadness in one person, do you know

what the dark looks like and that it has its own
gravity and how once I started taking anti-depressants
and finally felt "normal sadness" I was amazed at my good
mood and amazed to know that people walk around every
day only having this little bit of hurt, and against
real depression it is practically glee and it has
been 7 years of pills but I don't want to stop because I am
afraid of the low place, which only comes every blue moon
but it's still paralyzing, it feels like a thrumming, loud, louder
then unbearable once I am the noise with deathly
thoughts but if I say them out loud and weep then it goes away
within 2 hours or so, and my partner wonders
what it is doing to my kidneys, but he's rarely seen me when I
can't get up and he would feel helpless against the deluge
and my saying I don't know when he asks What is wrong? It is
my brain and he would have to watch me slope and be darkly.

III

The Unbeliever

For the first time from my mouth, I say *pray*
for us assuming she gospels in a god and
offering I do, too. Trundled syllable, I am a
con—cowed by the brute strength

belief takes, sight unseen. Grave bravery
to count on invisible untouchable myth. *Pray for*
us from my most shallow pocket, knowing I
need her faith to carry me, and who is it

that trusts a whole body bears us out, its
largest hands marbling unbelievers under
multilingual incantations?

Who is it that harbors kindling for the
pastor's devoted mouth, mirrors the evergreen
hunger of congregations' hands, giving up

the body to be taken holy elsewhere? Truth be
told, there's no proof, just people borne *back*
from half-light, from the optic nerve's most
mischievous macular halos.

There are no good answers for trauma, only
He'll never give you more than you can bear, which is
a bald-faced lie. He does, everyday, failings too
cacophonous to count. There's no good

reason why, if He is to be believed, He won't
sweep His want across the anathema to set it
right.

My Home Having Come to This

In the porn factory, none locks her head in a box. None is trapezed or gagged. Everyone wants to know what my inside looks like. And a transparency about the skin. It is not long before one stops his hinged posture and says, "Look at me. I love you," which my whole body opens to hear, as if it has been uttered before by someone I loved. I give myself as I've given myself to a field at dusk—without distraction or thought. Here. My body, my body's inside. Here. All its tender. Red pulp.

When She Is Looking Mean and Impressive

He asks if her nipples are pink, during which her body arrives to barter,
shifts from hand to hand. She gives what egg she has and

breaks into a jigger of pins.

How she is happening. How *is* she happening?
Her skin come away on his fingertips. His panic at having petted— if
that organ then others, too.
She is parts managed
toward the best idea of whole.

When She Is Looking Mean and Impressive

Thirsted to and paraded from. She gives her form to be made. She is
filled with song and asks to be choked. Becomes hungered and
talks about it for days. Her feeling she is owed dark.

Pulls charred wick with her fingers then fingers to
her mouth. Her blackened tongue.
Narratives for consumption marked
by a heedless draw toward currants.

She can't know it yet, but she will be so shearing.

Elegy for a Server

Tended by men, she tied herself in sailor's knots with silks, time-
lapsed through trapeze, and bent her parts into tiny boxes for his
liking to

       Look! Look!

She whispers to herself and watches all film ever framed where only
women swallow food into flush mouths, and there grows a liking
these telescopic basking bodies, electric Faberge

eggs, wands for wending along her labia. After years of calling lovers
by their motorcycles or truly mad eyes, she calls on her own body and
evenings begin redly, her broadening as fruit,

as monarchs shuddering at the dampened start. She has taken
everything she desires from bastard bodies and discards those weevils
on tarred roads. When she is having herself,

her self is the one she needs and she knows the softness of palm
under bite, apertures of her legs listing for light, breasts banked by
sweat. She knows what it tastes like to taste her.

Ownership, Play

I am property   an inlet.

I am what, tonight, you want: collar, hip, and unbound giving; given

toward arrangement. Veil-less, biological nod. There,

a palm I asked for. There, a bite I begged. Play,

against which I clot

to affirm you, your goodness.

I am Warm, I Know Nothing

It's true that you forget the voice of your sister. And her smell, so
imprinted, gets up in your dreaming and   Leathe's wick tide takes
that, too.

Her absence wakes something blackly in you
and, in the first months,
worn clothes and enfolded necks of
animals can be spread for her scent, hard
inhalations of her *having been.*

Sometimes you go about
the house proving she existed
through artifacts including her hand
in the lead script
of notebooks.
You see she wasn't a dream
although time tries to make her that way.

To Be Saved

The signs begin incrementally. Smally they plum

        then dilate under the skin as egg

so that we are forced to acknowledge each incident—

        sometimes very human—

the body shepherding itself to the bathroom in the night and

        back again, gasping where a toe smashes into the bed's

simple feet. For a moment, we wake to radiant pain opening

        as pure sound. Sometimes very metal—

There is worry that proliferates like operatic

        throats. Signs happen such that

We are always gasping and awakening.

NOTES

"The Lovers" is written in homage to Dorrianne Laux's poem of the
same name.

"The Unbeliever" title is borrowed from Elizabeth Bishop's poem of
the same name.

"The Wait" is written in homage to Elizabeth Bishop's "Casabianca"

"To Be in Love" is a golden shovel poem after "Gay Chaps at the Bar"
by Gwendolyn Brooks

"Elegy for a Server" contains phrasing from Elizabeth Bishop's
"Faustina or Rock Roses"

"I Am Warm, I Know Nothing" title from phrasing in Tsering Wangmo
Dhompa's poem "A Transitive"

ACKNOWLEDGEMENTS

Heavy thanks to the editors of the following journals and anthologies, who have sought to publish work from this collection: *Poetry, Best American Experimental Writing Anthology, CURA, The Account, Court Green, Columbia Poetry Review, Southern Indiana Review, Evening Will Come, The Equalizer, Indiana Review, Revising the Psalm: Work Celebrating the Writing of Gwendolyn Brooks, and The Golden Shovel Anthology.*

   My thanks also to Yaddo and the Trask's tending estate where several of these poems were created; Djerassi Foundation where many of these poems were revised; James Burroughs for your calls to ask "How's the writing going"; Douglas Kearney for responding to verse sent via text messages; to Chuck Kinder and Diane Cecily for your hot hearts for early drafts of the book; Sean Singer for your kind reading eyes and always clearest insight; Van Jordan for supporting your sister with filmic attention to the word; Laverne and Robert Burroughs for the reverence you give my writing time, and for the love that we pass between us; my cuzzo Caleb for asking, at 5, if poems have to rhyme, for letting me transcribe his first poem, and for saying he would put a "z" on the end of Stars "to make it cool"; graciousness to all those willing to talk with me about spirituality for the God Letter series of poems; Jeffrey Levine for intuiting what was possible beyond the wall; Kazim Ali for your devoted reading and giftable peace; Jim Schley for your solid suggestions; The Poetry Foundation, where I debuted many of these poems; Steve Young for your levity and our shared devotion to the fountain pen; Nikki Spigner, kin and reader extraordinaire; my supportive colleagues at Columbia College Chicago; all the institutions that have welcomed me for readings and talks, and your students who've read into my work; and, lastly, to all the books that poets are daring to write that insist on my sight. Thank you.

Printed in the USA
CPSIA information can be obtained
at www.ICGtesting.com
LVHW040537010624
781840LV00006B/134

9 781946 482389